Presented as a (an)

_____
(gift, seed, encouragement, edification, etc.)

for

_____

&

_____

on

_____

THE WINNING SERIES:
marriage

Casey & Whitney
Tillis
Delicia Gipson

LWPH

© Copyright © 2024, by Whitney Gipson-Tillis, Casey Tillis, Delicia Gipson. All rights reserved.

info@agapeoutlook.life

© All rights reserved. The copyright laws of the United States of America protect this book. This book may not be copied or reprinted for commercial gain or profit. The use of short quotations or occasional page copying for personal, or small group study is permitted. Upon written request, certain permission for use outside these limitations may be granted. No part of this publication may be reproduced, distributed, or transmitted in any form or by any means, including photocopying, recording, or other electronic or mechanical methods, without the publisher's prior written permission, except as permitted by U.S. copyright law. For permission requests, email Living Waters Publishing House at info@agapeoutlook.life.

Scripture quotations marked (NLT) are taken from the Holy Bible, New Living Translation, copyright © 1996, 2004, 2007 by Tyndale House Foundation and used by permission of Tyndale House Publishers, Inc., Carol Stream, Illinois 60188. All rights reserved.

Scripture quotations marked (AMP) are taken from the Amplified Bible copyright © 1954, 1958, 1962, 1964, 1965, 1987, and 2015 by the Lockman Foundation. All rights reserved. Used by permission.

Scripture quotations marked (NKJV) are taken from the New King James Version Bible copyright © 1982. Used by permission. All rights reserved.

Scripture quotations marked (KJV) are taken from the King James Bible. This translation is considered part of the public domain.

Book Cover design by Identity Amplified

ISBN 978-1-964450-00-1

Table of Contents

Let's Get Acquainted -------------------------- 23

God is NOT Optional -------------------------- 27

Undefiled ------------------------------------33

Needs --41

Expectation ----------------------------------47

Hers--55

His---73

Are You an Expert---------------------------- 89

Expect Repairs-------------------------------93

Ours---99

As We Part Ways ----------------------------127

Love Affirmations ----------------------------- 129

Check the Scale -------------------------------135

Appendix 1: Submission in Love---------------139

Appendix 2: Good or Garbage----------------155

Appendix 3: One Cord------------------------167

Feelings are not a GPS. They are a barometer to measure the current atmospheric conditions of your situation.

~Whitney Gipson-Tillis

To Liam, Adonis, Adara, Ava, Avery, and Alayna

for propelling us into the best versions of ourselves. And for being thirsty sponges soaking up everything you see and hear. Let our Christ-like examples propel you into the phenomenal individuals God loaned to us for such a time as this!

No one loves you more than us...except God, Himself.

Foreword

What an honor it is to shepherd, in the role of Pastor, the Tillis and Gipson families for more than a decade. This family has triumphantly overcome the struggles of singleness and, to this day, courageously tackles the countless challenges that come with marriage and family. These writers fear the Lord. The awe-inspired reverence of God is the preeminent factor in successfully breaking every chain of limitation and surmounting every road-blocking barrier put in place to destroy both their marriage and their lives. They have decided, together, to glorify God in all that they do (1 Corinthians 10:31, KJV).

Regret is not a word in the Tillis' lexicon. They lead their home and walk their step-by-step journey with the words uttered, bravely by Joshua in ancient history, "But if you refuse to serve the Lord, then choose today whom you will serve. Would you prefer the gods your ancestors served beyond the Euphrates? Or will it be the gods of the Amorites in whose land you now live? But as for me and my family, we will serve the Lord." Joshua 24:15 (NLT).

Instead of waiting for calamity and disaster, they govern their lives with thoughtful preventive measures. They strive to impart into their marriage and their children the necessity of submission, both to God and to each other. They lead by example and model Christ before all.

Before their July 2013 marriage, they sat with me and studiously gathered prevention principles, kingdom concepts, and diligently sought God during many premarital counseling sessions. All apply before and after the "I do". Fast forward to today when Casey and Whitney Tillis and accompanied by Whitney's mother, Delicia Gipson, submit to you, and the world, the same biblical prevention principles that will, undoubtedly, bless marriages and families around the world.

May the Lord bless and protect your marriage. May the Lord smile on your marriage and be gracious to you. May the Lord show you His favor and give you peace. Numbers 6:24-26 (NLT). Amen.

~Dr. Darrick Fields

Foreword

Are you ready to experience a rejuvenation in your marriage? Well, the Tillis' have done an amazing job in offering tools to help you achieve just that! As a Licensed Marriage and Family Therapist, I was thrilled to see the accuracy that is depicted in this book. I have come to know the Tillis' through ministry as we serve in the same church, Life-Changing Word Church, Team USA. It has been an honor to witness the example the Tillis' have shown, themselves, in their marriage. Throughout the years of knowing this family, their light and dedication to the purpose for their life has shined so bright, that you cannot help but to marvel at the impact it has made to those who surround them. So, I am not surprised that they decided to write a book.

Throughout EVERY chapter of this book, I found myself replaying similar scenarios I've encountered from those I treat in my private practice. Relatable content that is sure to provoke self-reflection and self-examination. Life-giving scriptures that support and provide credibility to their words. Their use of metaphors to illustrate the practicality of their tools will lead you to the curiosity you need to give it a try.

It is never too late to relearn your partner. If your relationship has been stale and stagnant, you are in dire need of rejuvenation! Allow this book to assist you to rekindle that which was loss. You deserve it!

-Kesia Fields, MS, LMFT;
Owner of Pivotal Change Counseling Service.

THE WINNING SERIES:
marriage

Let's Get Acquainted

Have you ever struggled to know the right gift to give your spouse? Did you settle on something you were unsure would appeal to them? This may have caused you to wish you knew your spouse better so you could show them how much they mean to you. The purpose of this book is to obliterate the guesswork so there is no more hoping and wishing and praying you got it right!

The sections of this book ask gentle, probing questions. Take your time, answering each question thoughtfully. She will answer "Hers," he will answer "His," and you both will answer "Ours." The questions are intended to spark conversation, generate curiosity, and reintroduce wonder into your relationship. It is not intended to create controversy; rather, it is an opportunity for you to be vulnerable, honest, and forthcoming.

If your first thought is *"But I told them this already,"* you may be right. During the early stages of a relationship, couples discuss a variety of subject matters. But honestly, how much of that do you remember? We all forget a detail or two, and, on top of that, we change over time. So, as you begin, open your heart to the idea that you have a wonderful opportunity to love each other more meaningfully.

We, the authors of this tool, love LOVE, and we want to see your love bloom like a mountainside full of flowers. When others encounter the two of you, we want them to see the beauty of your thriving relationship and long to follow your example! Let us help you discover how your marriage can bloom. Together, rekindle the fire you once had—or ignite a new one! This book was ordained by God to help your love grow! Look at how good God is! He is love, so, of course, He loves LOVE, too!

Faith and fear cannot occupy the same space.

~Delicia Gipson

God is NOT Optional

God is not optional! In one sentence, we shine a light on the single most important idea to take away from this book: God must always be the highest priority in your relationship. Revelation 3:15–16 (NLT) admonishes, "I know all the things you do, that you are neither hot nor cold. I wish that you were one or the other! But since you are like lukewarm water, neither hot nor cold, I will spit you out of my mouth!"

The first priority must be to cultivate a strong relationship with God, both as individuals and as a couple.

Relationships fail for many reasons, but fear is a major contributor. Do any of the following thoughts seem familiar?

"We will always be broke."

"Once a cheater, always a cheater!"

"My relationship will never change."

Fear has a powerful impact on all relationships: with God, with your spouse, with your children, with anyone. Bear in mind, that 1 John 4:18 (NKJV) says there is no fear in love. With this understanding, your marriage is likely to suffer because of fear. Ask yourself: Is there fear in my marriage? If so, why? What can be done to remove this fear? Somewhere in the depths of yourself, the light of God's unfailing love has yet to shine. These fears cannot abide simultaneously in a loving marriage. Fear may manifest as sadness, defensiveness, resentment, or as an "I told you so." response. Such manifestations reveal places where you can still invite God into your relationship.

When people board an airplane, the flight attendant holds up the oxygen mask, demonstrates the proper use of it, and instructs all parents to put their masks on before assisting their small children.

Failing to prioritize your health and safety is not a selfish act; rather, it shows you want to be able to help those you love. Similarly, putting God first shows you want to ensure success in your marriage!

The way you put your marriage relationship's mask on is by going to God in prayer together, by studying God's word together, and by worshiping together—regularly. Invite God into all the spaces of your relationship. Even if you think the tasks at hand—such as changing diapers, changing the oil, or making dinner—is mundane, invite God into it. Cultivating this habit will prove fruitful in your personal life and your marriage. Proverbs 3:5-6 (NLT) says, "Trust in the Lord with all your heart; do not depend on your own understanding. Seek His will in all you do, and He will show you which path to take." God desires to reside in the deepest, most intimate places of your relationship. Submit to His desires! Give Him free reign to dwell in your communication, your finances, and even your bedroom.

You have to be something before you can become something.

~Casey Tillis

Undefiled

God gave you your marriage in its Eden state. Will you keep it, or will you, like Adam and Eve, defile it? Now, examine your relationship with sex both the act and the intimacy connected to it.

The Intimacy.

Throughout life, hormonal and bodily changes can create curiosity and tension. Left unaddressed, people, young and old, married and single, can stumble into sexual sin, unaware.

The entertainment industry glorifies sex as a way to gain power, happiness, wealth, and satisfaction. Many types of couples are displayed that, are by no means, aligned with God's design for marriage. God calls for one man and one woman to be fruitful, multiply, replenish, subdue, and have dominion for a lifetime (Genesis 1:28 KJV).

God fully endorses sex, sexual acts, and sexuality within the constraints of His commands. Sex brings married couples as close to heaven as they can come while here on earth. God's purpose for sex in marriage is for partners to give freely; after all, God loves a cheerful giver. If both partners give, both partners' needs will be completely satisfied.

You are blessed by God with this marriage. He granted you certain authority and declared you fruitful. He equipped you to fill your home and to govern it. You have dominion. Like Adam and Eve, God has presented you with the choice of how to manage it.

As a believer, make no room in your dominion for the enemy to come in through infidelious things such as pornography or other extra-marital sexual interests. 1 Corinthians 7:5 (NLT) says, "Do not deprive each other of sexual relations unless you both agree to refrain from sexual intimacy for a limited time so you can give yourselves more completely to prayer.

Afterward, you should come together again so that Satan won't be able to tempt you because of your lack of self-control."

The Act

If you were not a virgin when you entered into your marriage, consider the concept of putting wine into wineskins. In ancient biblical times, fresh wine was poured into new wineskins so that the wine and the skin aged together. If new wine had been poured into old wineskins, the aged skin would not have the same integrity and would burst.

In this case, the old wineskin is your mindset about sex and the old wine is your sexual history before you entered into this marriage. Pouring the new wine of your marital relationship into the old wineskin is unwise, as is thinking the old wine appears better. The new wine of your current marriage needs time to age and mature. Read Luke 5:37-39 and ask for revelation from the Holy Spirit in this.

Renew your mind and take the time to learn from one another. Invite God in as He is the author of your love story. Let your lovemaking go from glory to glory. The grass is only greener where you water it, so water your Eden.

Your intent must match your impact.

~Kesia Fields

Needs

As we launch into deeper water, we must discuss needs and expectation. Sometimes, these two are interchanged. Allowing them to maintain a separate place in your relationship is paramount.

Remember these things:
1. Unmet needs can adversely impact the ability of a spouse to meet current and future needs of the other.
2. A lack of emotional development can create internal and relational conflict.

A baby who cries, poops, eats, and sleeps scores 100% when being measured by infant behavioral standards. If this baby were measured by adult standards, however, this infant would fall short. It is important to maintain the proper perspective when considering your performance in the marriage relationship.

A baby is unable to communicate his needs because, developmentally, he cannot speak, or even comprehend the moment-to-moment changes happening. All we hear are baby cries. In the same way, an adult who cannot identify the root cause of pain may also act out in aggression, overwhelming tears, or retreat within him or herself. If you were not afforded the tools or the safe opportunities to experience, describe, and then express the myriads of your emotions, you may still be unable to do much more than cry. The feelings may be overpowering. You may not have a very sophisticated emotional vocabulary. The only thing you know is something hurts or is uncomfortable or sparks memories of distress. We must recognize if we are dealing with someone's wounded inner child rather than an adult who has a fully capable and adequately developed identity.

Have you ever conducted an inventory on your level of patience, your self-control, or your meekness? These qualities are only a sample of what is needed in the evaluation of your capacity. If you go to the market, regardless of the items needed, the amount of money you have to spend is finite. In the same way, each individual has a finite amount of individual resources. Your capacity is yours, alone. 2 Corinthians 9:7 (NLT) teaches us, "You must each decide in your heart how much to give. And don't give reluctantly or in response to pressure. "For God loves a person who gives cheerfully."" As you consider what you give in your relationship, decide how much you will give and to what degree. Your spouse must also decide how much to give without reluctance or compulsion. It would be unwise to spend more than the finiteness of your capacity. Choose carefully. If we expect no more of an infant than he or she can offer, the same grace must be extended to your spouse regarding emotional maturity, time, affection, strength, or any individual resource he or she has as it plays a very crucial role in all relationship dynamics. See "Check the Scale" to determine your capacity as often as is needed.

If narrow is the way, there is no room for error.

~Sarah Olea

expect

Expectation

If, in my mind, I think my spouse will produce 100, but my spouse only produces 60, my expectation was inappropriate. My imagination (2 Corinthians 10:5, NLT) created a standard that my spouse would not, and perhaps could not, meet. If the expectation was only in my mind, how would my spouse know what I expected? How would my spouse know, for example, that I was expecting him to buy a ham at the grocery store, pick up clothes at the dry cleaners, and then come home and watch the kids if I never verbalized it? Could anything good come from this?

God is for relationships. Relate, the root of the word relationship, means to bring into or establish association, connection, or relation. In the diagram, we show the proper elements for the foundation of your relationship as love, trust, and communication.

Effective communication is generated in an environment of trust. An environment of trust can only be produced where love is the goal. Because the "greatest of these is love (1 Corinthians 13:13, NLT).

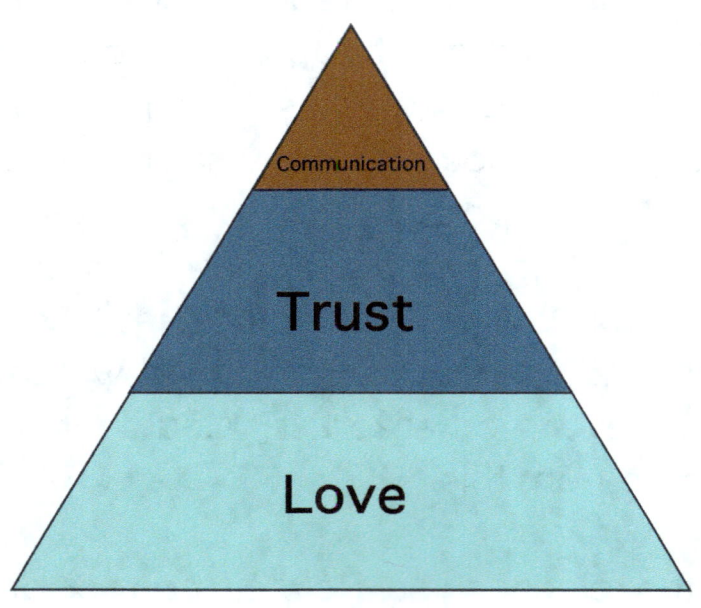

Imagine how hard relationships would be if one person created rules for the other without sharing them. How would they communicate, trust, or love well? Having inappropriate expectation for one's partner creates disappointment and resentment , which can turn into deep-seated anger. For those upon whom the expectation is placed, feelings of confusion and anxiety can develop.

Expectation, in and of itself, is not bad. Inappropriate or unexpressed expectation can be debilitating, however. Think about expectation for a moment. What exactly is it you want in your relationship? Do you want a departing hug and kiss? Ask for it. Do you want your sweetheart to take you out on a date? Suggest an activity. Are you tired of answering "What's for dinner today?" Suggest a restaurant you and your spouse love. The bottom line is to be deliberate in communicating your expectation. Your spouse cannot read minds any better than you can, so don't beat around the bush or drop hints. Who can read minds? Jesus. The Holy Spirit. God. Neither you nor your spouse can do this.

1 Peter 3:1-2 (NLT) tells us this: "In the same way, you wives must accept the authority of your husbands. Then, even if some refuse to

obey the Good News, your godly lives will speak to them without any words. They will be won over by observing your pure and reverent lives." Many Christian spouses claim their actions are pure and reverent; however, their actions are steeped in expectation. As a result, frustration grows exponentially as they see no change in their spouse's behaviors. Instead of walking by faith, what they see determines what they believe. Philippians 1:6 (NLT) says"… God, who began a good work within you, will continue His work until it is finally finished on the day when Christ Jesus returns." The work of changing your partner's heart began when you began to pray. Remember, that there is nothing you can do but pray and lead a pure and reverent life before your spouse. Only God will finish the work, so trade in your expectation in your spouse for expectancy in God's word.

Above all else, our anticipation and expectation should be laser-focused on God's ability to exceed our wildest imaginations. Yielding ourselves fully to Him helps us communicate our expectation to our spouse. Meeting God's expectation and communicating in His love will create a home filled with peace and joy.

Consider this:
Have you placed expectation on another?
Yes ☐   No ☐

Please describe an example.
_____
_____
_____
_____

Has expectation been placed on you?
Yes ☐ No ☐

Please describe an example.
_____
_____
_____
_____

A fall may happen. A fail is when we choose to stay fallen.

~Delicia Gipson

Hers

Many individuals enter marriage with preconceived notions of what they believe it should be without expressing those ideas or receiving feedback from their partner. This creates cracks in the foundation of the relationship as failure to communicate leaves room for misunderstanding, confusion, and division. In Matthew 7:24 (NLT), Jesus teaches us to build our home—including relationships—on bedrock instead of sand because storms are unavoidable. A house built on preconceived notions will encounter a great fall because it was built on a shaky foundation.

While still dating, I gave my future husband a clear idea of what I wanted in a marriage. I intentionally shared the idea that I wanted my husband, whoever he may be, to be home every night to tuck the kids into bed. While not a deal breaker, it was a very high priority for me. Now, the only reality my children know is that their dad is always there for them.

After getting married, my emotional immaturity revealed itself. Triggers from past trauma would cause me to shut down emotionally. With God's help, I examined this area and began to grow. While I am not perfect, the work I have done has benefited me personally, my husband, our marriage, and our children. Dealing with my triggers was my responsibility. Once I learned how to communicate with myself, I could better communicate with my husband.

Like every other woman, I experience hormonal changes. My gracious husband makes room for these, honoring me as the weaker vessel (1 Peter 3:7, NLT). But because my husband does not want to live in the corner of the rooftop due to having a quarrelsome wife (Proverbs 25:24, NLT), I have to make room for him to be able to live comfortably IN the house with me. A woman is defined as a helper because her role resembles that of the Holy Spirit (John 14:26 NKJV, Genesis 2:18 NKJV).

A woman makes a difference in a home and a family. Before she comes, the house is bland, uncoordinated, and maybe even unkempt. A wife adds life and spirit to a home even before there are children because women are givers. Woman, what do you have to give to your home? There are many answers to this question. One woman may be a great cook, another a skilled organizer, and another may create ambiance through being spatially adept. All women have something great to give to their husbands and their home!

In marriage, he gives, she gives—everyone gives! Through partnership with our spouse, we imitate God's original plan for the husband–wife relationship created in the world's infancy.

Ultimately, the goal of husband and wife is to out-serve the other. If he takes care of the laundry without being asked, she can draw his bath and help him unwind from the day. If we are busy serving each other, there will be no time to nitpick.

In the end, we must allow Colossians 3:23 NLT and 1 Corinthians 10:31 NLT to remind us that when we serve our spouse, we serve the Lord.

Communicating our desires to each other eliminates moving targets and allows us to enter into the rest God created for marriage. Ladies, answer the following questions with thoughtfulness, hope, and love. It will help to create a fresh fire in your marriage and recreate the giddiness you once relished.

~Whitney

Her Favorites

Pass time: _____

Color: _____

Movie: _____

Flower: _____

Music Genre: _____

Song: _____

Restaurant: _____

Breakfast: _____

Lunch: _____

Dinner: _____

Snack: _____

Sweet treat: _____

Stress Relief Package: _____

Travel destination: _____

Store: _____

Designer: _____

Car: _____

Other favorite things?
_____
_____
_____
_____

Her Mysteries Revealed

Birthdate: _____

My primary love language is _____

The ideal way to celebrate my birthday is_____
_____
_____

The perfect birthday gift for me is _____
_____

Ring size: _____

Shoe size:_____

Blouse size:_____

Pants size: _____

Dress size: _____

Bra size:_____

Frugal or extravagant spender? _____

Gym rat or couch potato?_____

Sneakers, heels, or flip-flops? _____

Warm & fuzzy or cool & prickly?_____

Romantic or practical? _____

The time of day I feel my best is_____
_____

The time of day I feel my worst is_____
_____

Just for fun, I would love to try_____
_____
_____
_____

For a quick outing, I would like to go to or do ___
_____
_____
_____

I think (insert a traveling adventure) _____
_____
_____ would be so exciting.

I would like to go or do (insert any activity) _____
_____
_____
_____for our anniversary.

These items are on my bucket list: _____
_____
_____

When I am sick, I might display these types of behaviors. _____
_____
_____
_____
_____

When I am sick, I want these (insert items or actions) _____
_____
_____
_____

When I am discouraged, I might display these types of behaviors. _____
_____
_____
_____

When I am discouraged, I want (insert items or actions) _____
_____
_____
_____

A Few More Details About Her

I am skilled or talented in the areas of _____
_____
_____
_____

My greatest accomplishment is_____
_____
_____
_____
_____

I find myself most challenged in the areas of___
_____
_____
_____
_____

I could use help growing in (insert any area) ___
_____
_____

My career goals are _____
_____
_____
_____

Five of my core values are _____
_____
_____
_____
_____
_____

I feel safe when _____
_____
_____
_____
_____

In a man, I am most attracted to _____
_____
_____

An ideal husband is one who _____
_____
_____
_____
_____
_____

An ideal marriage is one where_____
_____
_____
_____
_____
_____
_____

I want my husband to lead by _____
_____
_____
_____
_____
_____

What I love most about my husband is _____
_____
_____
_____
_____
_____
_____
_____
_____
_____

(Read and re-read this when situations are challenging.)

I would like to have _____ children.

I am open to adoption or surrogacy.

Yes ☐   No ☐

I am open to a prenuptial agreement

Yes ☐   No ☐

Dying to yourself, you will always look like Christ.

~Whitney Gipson-Tillis

His

Brothers, welcome to your journey of becoming a compassionate and thoughtful partner. I am hopeful that this manual will help you become a blessing to your girlfriend, fiancé, or wife.

Firstly, this tool is yours. Highlight it. Write all over it. Tailor what is provided to suit your journey, adjusting the course of your relationship with this tool as a compass. When storms greatly trouble the waters of your relationship, when the night is long and penetrating, when the ship of your relationship drifts off course, return to these words to guide you like a North Star. This book will help you recalibrate your thoughts and behaviors.

To be clear, nothing about a relationship with a woman is as difficult as the world suggests. Though there are differences in the way men and women are fulfilled in relationships, we can ground ourselves and create a unique harmony. God created men and women in specific, purposeful ways. Unfortunately, the pervasive influence of this world has clouded our view of His design. As men, we have a divine responsibility to protect, provide for, and lead our wives and children (Ephesians 5:25-26 NKJV), holding tightly to the helm even when secular culture says men should surrender.

Understanding is the cornerstone of clear communication. As you become a more capable leader in your home, consider your role, her role, and the responsibilities you both share.

As you work through this manual, if you discover other information that is helpful for strengthening your relationship, add it in. This is your tool! Improve your covenant relationship with tips and tricks that meet your needs. Take time to intentionally listen to her, always remembering the commitment you made to her (Genesis 2:24 NKJV).

~Casey

His Favorites

Pass time: _____

Color: _____

Movie: _____

Flower: _____

Music Genre: _____

Song: _____

Restaurant: _____

Breakfast: _____

Lunch: _____

Dinner: _____

Snack: _____

Sweet treat: _____

Stress Relief Package: _____

Travel destination: _____

Store: _____

Designer: _____

Car: _____

Other favorite things?
_____

_____

_____

_____

His Mysteries Revealed

Birthdate: _____

My primary love language is _____

The ideal way to celebrate my birthday is_____
_____
_____
_____

The perfect birthday gift for me is _____
_____
_____

Ring size: _____

Shoe size: _____

Neck size: _____

Arm length: _____

Pants size: _____

Caps: Fitted, Velcro, or Snapback _____

Cufflinks: Yes ☐ No ☐

Frugal or extravagant spender _____

Gym rat or couch potato? _____

Sneakers, dress shoes, or flip-flops? _____

Warm & fuzzy or cool & prickly? _____

Romantic or practical? _____

The time of day I feel my best is _____

The time of day I feel my worst is _____

Just for fun, I would love to try
_____
_____
_____

For a quick outing, I would like to go to or do___
_____
_____
_____

I think (insert a traveling adventure) _____
_____
_____ would be so exciting.

I would like to go or do (insert any activity)_____
_____
_____
_____for our anniversary.

These items are on my bucket list:_____
_____
_____

When I am sick, I might display these types of behaviors._____
_____
_____
_____
_____

When I am sick, I want (insert items or actions)_____
_____
_____
_____

When I am discouraged, I might display these types of behaviors._____
_____
_____
_____

When I am discouraged, I want (insert items or actions)_____
_____
_____
_____

A Few More Details About Him

I am skilled or talented in the areas of _____

My greatest accomplishment is_____

I find myself most challenged in the areas of___

I could use help growing in (insert any area)____

My career goals are_____
_____
_____
_____

Five of my core values are_____
_____
_____
_____

I feel safe when_____
_____
_____
_____
_____
_____

In a woman, I am most attracted to _____
_____
_____
_____

An ideal wife is one who _____
_____
_____
_____
_____
_____

An ideal marriage is one where _____
_____
_____
_____
_____
_____

I would love to lead my wife by _____
_____
_____
_____
_____
_____

What I love most about my wife is_____
_____
_____
_____
_____
_____
_____
_____
_____
_____

(Read and re-read this when situations are challenging.)

I would like to have _____ children.

I am open to adoption or surrogacy.

Yes ☐   No ☐

I am open to a prenuptial agreement

Yes ☐   No ☐

Job

Documents reputa

training has a general

-job training takes place aw

employee does not count a

has the **Expert** dvantage

oroughly on the training itself. This

ting concepts and ideas.

ffers from exercise in that people of impr

Goals

ormance

Pursue peace, not problems

~Dr. Darrick Fields

Are You an Expert?

Because many people hit milestones around the same age or stage of life, we tend to assume that everyone will. For example, we assume a five-year-old should know how to tie his shoes, a 16-year-old should know how to drive a car, and a 21-year-old should know how to handle drinking alcohol. However, this is not always the case for everyone. Neurological capacity and life experiences can affect readiness. At the tender age of three, our neurodivergent child excelled in mathematics. At five years old, he spoke three languages. At eight, he could recall the names of all 50 U.S. states and their capitals. At nine he could recite all the books of the Bible. Despite having such intellect, he still struggles with tying his shoes at the age of 10. We have learned that age does not always correlate with ability. Your relationship expertise is similar to this. Maybe you have only been together a short while or maybe you have been an item for many years.

Regardless, resist the temptation to assume you have reached an expert status in your relationship. Rather, embrace the idea of being a lifelong learner. As time passes, the two of you may mature at different rates. Reality may be different from what you expected. Your life together in the fifth year of marriage may be more developed in some ways and less so in others. The key is to be gracious toward one another.

Consider this:
How do I know if or when to extend grace to my partner? How can I do this? What if I don't want to? When situations arise that frustrate you, go back and reread this book. Use The Winning Series: Marriage in conjunction with Bible reading and prayer to find the answers you need. As a declaration of faith, proclaim "It is easy to love!"

Are you communicating or just wording?

~Delicia Gipson

Expect Repairs

In any relationship, specifically in marriage, confusion, assumption, and expectation are traps! These fiery darts are launched to destroy your marriage. How do we prepare for such attacks? Ephesians 6:12 (NKJV) describes how spiritual attacks wreak havoc in our world. Inside your marriage, they can do lasting damage if not addressed head on. Communication, health conditions, and finances are some areas where couples may need to do spiritual warfare; without it, these biting blows can leave couples feeling dazed and uncertain about the future.

That uncertainty can lead to disagreements, criticism, and resentment. Criticism is often ineffective because it puts people on the defensive and possibly even spurs them to tune out. However, carefully considered words of encouragement accompanied by thoughtful feedback is more likely to be well-received.

Spouses need encouragement in the growth process. The biblical approach to conflict resolution is the best method to use. Matthew 18:15 (NLT) states, "if another believer sins against you, go privately, and point out the offense. If the other person listens and confesses it, you have won that person back." This verse gives us hope that damaged relationships can be restored. All married couples should expect to make repairs from time to time; these are possible through the redemptive power of Jesus Christ.

After a disagreement, let emotion cool down; then come back together and talk about the matter as adults who love God and one another (Ephesians 4:26, NLT). Knowing that we all fall short of the glory of God (Romans 3:23, NLT), discern the spiritual influences at play. Provide feedback and express concerns, all while being responsive to the guidance of the Spirit Who does not want you to hurt your spouse by handling sensitive subject matter carelessly.

Galatians 6:1 (NLT) admonishes, "... gently and humbly help that person back onto the right path. And be careful not to fall into the same temptation yourself."

Anatomically speaking, we have two ears and only one mouth. If we use our ears twice as much as our mouths, we will be a shining example of James 1:19 (NLT): "Understand this, my dear brother and sisters: You must all be quick to listen, slow to speak, and slow to get angry." Being quick to listen means seeking understanding. Being slow to speak means accepting the critique and responding appropriately. As adults and mature believers, we should be able to handle criticism delivered with care by the ones who love us most. However, Proverbs 18:19 (NLT) warns, "An offended friend is harder to win back than a fortified city. Arguments separate friends like a gate locked with bars." When we are angered or embarrassed when confronted by our shortcomings, it is very easy to be offended. So, how can we move from a place of pride to a place of humility? The book of Proverbs provides a blueprint for course correction, and that correction may be the salvation of your marriage. Making repairs in a relationship, though challenging, is a worthy endeavor.

There is nothing you can do to remove yourself from the unfailing, never-ending, love of God, who designed the marriage relationship. He set the rules: wives are to submit to husbands who love them as Christ loves the church (Ephesians 5:22, 25 NKJV). Spouses, remember when you speak that there is a stark contrast between talking **at each other** and talking **to each other**. If the ship of your marriage has taken on water and you feel as though it is sinking, perform repairs! Because God knows what is best and His goodness is available to you, He will perform the work that is needed. Though God may not work the way you expect, remain open to his ways. Remember that we are commanded to love one another and be patient as God mends your relationship.

We are fruitful, we multiply, we subdue, we replenish and we have dominion!

~ Whitney Gipson-Tillis

Ours

This section invites you both to be vulnerable. Just as gardens need to be nurtured, so does your marriage. Though you have answered many questions about yourselves as individuals, it is time to bravely launch into deep waters—together.

Revelation 3:20 (NLT) says "Look! I stand at the door and knock. If you hear my voice and open the door, I will come in, and we will share a meal together as friends." Jesus demonstrates his love for us by waiting to be invited into our hearts. While trust and respect are earned, love is a gift! Now is the time for you to consciously allow your partner into the depths of your heart.

God's grace is sufficient for your relationship (2 Corinthians 12:9, NKJV). Just as we are apt to be gracious to ourselves when we make mistakes, we must rely on the Holy Spirit to give that same grace to our loved one. 1 Peter 4:8 (AMP) reminds us that love extends the grace that is necessary for relational longevity.

God's vision for marriage is as follows:
- Two people become one unit in the covenant relationship of marriage (Genesis 2:24, AMP, Matthew 19:5-6, NKJV).

- This union is not to be broken by divorce (Mark 10:9, NKJV).

- Husband love your wife in a Christ-like manner, and wife submit to your husband as you do to the Lord. (Ephesians 5:22-29, AMP)

- Your vision for your marriage must align with God's. If it does not, you welcome division. Together, write your vision, making it plain, so that you may walk it out in harmony.

~Casey & Whitney

Our Relationship Monuments

When and where was our first date? _____
_____
_____

When and where was our first kiss? _____
_____
_____
_____
_____

When did we decide to exclusively belong to each other? _____
_____
_____

When and where did our marriage proposal take place? _____
_____
_____
_____
_____

Our Separate Histories

What were our lives like growing up? Discuss key family structures that enriched or challenged our lives.

How were household responsibilities divided in our childhood homes? How did we feel about those systems?

One Cord

A vision for our life together.

What are our personality types? In what ways are we similar or different? Discuss the dynamics of how our personalities will converge as we encounter challenges, surprises, set up routines, etc._____

_____
_____
_____
_____
_____
_____
_____
_____
_____
_____
_____
_____
_____
_____

What would we like to do or accomplish together as a couple/ family? (Think of this as your collective bucket list.)

What does quality time look like as a **couple**? This is something we will do both before and after we have children.

What does quality time look like as a **family**? Here, think about what we will do as a family to build healthy and happy memories.

What kind of life do we want to provide for ourselves and our children? What type of home, cars, and general standard of living are we aiming for?

Let's talk about parenting together. Let's talk about what type of parents we are (or will be).

What role will each of us play in earning household income?

How will we manage our finances? Discuss budgeting, bill paying, and spending.

If we decide to, when would be the ideal time for us to have children?_____
_____
_____
_____
_____
_____
_____
_____
_____

How many will we have?_____

What parenting style will we use? (Refer to pros and cons from your own childhoods and agree on key principles for raising children). _____

_____
_____
_____
_____
_____
_____
_____
_____
_____
_____
_____
_____
_____
_____
_____
_____
_____

Do we want to have pets? Yes ☐   No ☐

If so, what kind and how many? _____

When should we acquire them? _____

Purchase or adopt? _____

Are there any reasons why we would surrender a pet?_____
_____
_____
_____
_____
_____
_____
_____
_____
_____
_____
_____
_____

What household responsibilities (e.g. laundry, cooking, dishes, etc.) will be borne by each of us?
_____
_____
_____
_____
_____
_____
_____
_____
_____
_____
_____
_____

Are there any tasks either of us absolutely do not want to do? If so, what are they? If we agree to perform a task initially but want to abdicate the responsibility later, how will we negotiate this?_____
_____
_____
_____
_____
_____
_____
_____
_____
_____
_____
_____

How near or far from family we will live (next door, across town, another city/state/country)?
_____
_____
_____
_____
_____
_____
_____
_____
_____
_____

Why do we want to have this amount of distance from our families? _____
_____
_____
_____
_____

One Cord

...to listen and to be heard.

(Putting on the mask of our relationship, together)

What are ways we think alike? How do we think differently? What do we do when we disagree? What is our plan for resolving disagreement? How long do we cool off, if needed? In whose hands does the final decision rest?

Let's talk about accountability. How do we hold one another accountable? How do we hold ourselves accountable?

What major medical histories do we or our extended families have?

If unable to communicate, how can we advocate for each other in dire situations with medical professionals, police, and other persons of authority? _____
_____
_____
_____
_____
_____
_____
_____
_____
_____
_____
_____
_____
_____
_____
_____
_____
_____
_____
_____

You're not qualified to disqualify yourself.

~Whitney Gipson-Tillis

As We Part Ways

As we have seen throughout this book, self-evaluation is a key to success. Use what you have learned here as frequently as necessary, even if that is on a moment-to-moment basis.

You are a work in progress and very deserving of love. Do you treat yourself with love when you oversleep? Are you patient with yourself when you make a mistake? Are you kind to yourself by scheduling a vacation when you need a break? Or is the voice in your head critical? We sometimes mistreat ourselves without a second thought. Consequently, we may mistreat our spouses, too, believing that our thoughts are true simply because they are familiar. Let this book be a reminder to keep "short accounts" of failures and missteps, whether they be yours or your partners'.

Below, you will find a simple, yet highly

effective exercise that should be read three times. Do not pass go or collect $200, as we learned playing the classic childhood game of Monopoly!

The first time you read it, insert your name in the blanks, affirming yourself. The second time, add your name to the blanks again, this time declaring your love for your spouse. The third time, add your spouse's name in the blanks declaring how your spouse loves you.

Recite this scripture every day for a month and watch how dramatically your view of yourself, your partner, and your relationship will align more with God's unfailing love.

Jesus came that we might have life and life more abundantly (John 10:10, NKJV). This abundant life includes your marriage. Expect the good seeds you plant in this relationship to produce good fruit.

Love Affirmations

----

endures with patience and serenity,

----

is kind and thoughtful,

and

----

is not jealous or envious;

----

does not brag and

----

is not proud or arrogant.

----

is not rude;

----

is not self-seeking,

_____
is not provoked [nor overly sensitive and easily angered];

_____
does not take into account a wrong endured.

_____
does not rejoice at injustice,

but, _____
rejoices with the truth [when right and truth prevail].

_____
bears all things [regardless of what comes],

_____
believes all things [looking for the best in each one],

_____ hopes all things [remaining steadfast during difficult times],

_____
endures all things [without weakening].

_____
never fails

_____
never fades nor ends].

But as for prophecies, they will pass away; as for tongues, they will cease; as for the gift of special knowledge, it will pass away.

For

_____
know(s) in part, and

_____
prophesy (prophesies) in part [for our knowledge is fragmentary and incomplete]. But when that which is complete and perfect comes, that which is incomplete and partial will pass away.

When

_____
was a child,

_____
talked like a child,

_____
thought like a child,

_____
reasoned like a child;
when

_____
became a man (an adult),

_____
did away with childish things. "

1 Corinthians 13 (AMP)

Check the Scale

On a scale of 0-10 (with 10 being full and zero is completely empty),

How full is my tank? _____

Do I struggle to identify the level of resources you can offer? _____

Ex. How much patience is in reserve after a day of work? How much patience do you have after a sleepless night with the baby?

What is my response if your spouse's score is low? _____

What is my response if my score is also low? _____

What can I do to increase my score? _____

What do I do if my score at the beginning of the day is low? _____

What are my needs? _____
_____
_____
_____
_____
_____
_____
_____

What do I do to meet them? _____
_____
_____
_____
_____
_____
_____
_____

Appendix 1

Submission in Love

We realize that some of our readers have been married for only a few years. You may have real-life experiences of what this exercise is presenting. So, why should you engage in this exercise? Under more controlled conditions, using the blank canvas of your imagination, and working as a team, you may develop a more loving approach than you would in real-life scenarios.

Now, it's time to display your acting skills! Role-play the following scenarios, and then record your experience.

SIL #1: Romantic Getaway

Wife:
Highly driven
Primary income source
Demanding job requires long hours and travel away from home for weeks at a time sometimes
Frequent interruptions at home

Husband:
Laid back
Earns some money doing special event photography
Manages the couple's joint bank account
Enjoys planning special trips as a couple

We:
Have set a strict budget

Husband: Wants to go to another country in late Summer or Fall

How was the conversation (good, bad, challenging, easy, etc.)?_____
_____
_____
_____
_____
_____
_____
_____

Did either of you have expectation? Did you express yours? _____
_____
_____
_____
_____
_____
_____
_____
_____
_____

Did either of you feel conflict arise? If so, how did you resolve it?_____
_____
_____
_____
_____
_____
_____
_____

Was there a resolution? If so, what was agreed upon? _____
_____
_____
_____
_____
_____
_____
_____
_____
_____
_____
_____

SIL #2: Joint Stewardship

Wife:
Primary income source
Manages the joint bank account

Husband:
Works for a non-profit
Transitioning to stay-at-home father of three adopted children

We:
Have a high debt-to-income ratio
Have a strict budget
Are in the process of adopting three children

Scenario: Wife wants to buy a top-of-the-line iMac computer without discussing it with husband first

How was the conversation (good, bad, challenging, easy, etc.)? _____
_____
_____
_____
_____
_____
_____
_____
_____
_____
_____
_____

Did you consider previous purchases that may affect the adoption process? *(According to USCIS, adoptive parents' household income must be equal to or higher than 125% of the US poverty level. For this scenario, the household size is 5 [Husband, Wife, and 3 children].)* Elaborate. _____

_____
_____
_____
_____
_____
_____
_____
_____

Did you consider how purchases may affect the adoption proceedings? Elaborate. _____

_____
_____
_____
_____
_____
_____
_____

How did the change in finances and family size impact your relationship? Elaborate. _____

_____
_____
_____
_____
_____
_____
_____
_____

Was there resolution? If so, what was agreed upon? _____

_____
_____
_____
_____
_____
_____
_____
_____

SIL #3: Touchdown!

Husband:
Primary income source

Wife:
Secondary income source
Manages the joint bank account

We:
Have a strict budget

Scenario: Without prior discussion with his wife, husband bought sky box season tickets to every game of his favorite sports team - including away games. He also plans to travel to the Super Bowl regardless of who is playing. Hopefully, his favorite team.

How was the conversation (good, bad, challenging, easy, etc.)? Describe the intensity of the emotions. _____
_____
_____
_____
_____
_____
_____
_____
_____

Have you explored any compromises (selling tickets, refunds, traveling together, etc.)? _____
_____
_____
_____
_____
_____
_____
_____
_____

Were you able to agree that this is Husband's Christmas gift for the next five years?

_____
_____
_____
_____
_____
_____
_____

Was there resolution? If so, what was agreed upon? _____

_____
_____
_____
_____
_____
_____
_____
_____
_____

SIL #4: Wife-preneur

Husband:
Only income source

Wife:
Manages the joint bank account
Stay-at-home wife

We:
have a strict budget

Scenario: She hasn't discussed it with her husband, but wife plans to launch a small business requiring the purchase of equipment, inventory, payroll, building lease, online store, and paying taxes. On top of the huge financial investment, the new business will require tons of time and energy.

How was the conversation (good, bad, challenging, easy, etc.)? _____
_____
_____
_____
_____

Were you able to manage emotions and expectation? _____
_____
_____
_____
_____

Understanding that businesses lose money initially, describe the plan you developed to gradually build the business. _____
_____
_____
_____
_____
_____
_____

Understanding that roles and responsibilities will have to change, what plans did you develop for managing the home while wife explores this business venture? _____
_____
_____
_____
_____
_____
_____
_____
_____
_____

Appendix 2

Good or Garbage

As a couple, how good are you at discerning Truth? Let's find out. Read each statement. Write "Good" or "Garbage" in the corresponding blank.

Special note: If you read it and it sounds good, it could still be garbage. These truths are based on the Word of God.

How many will you answer correctly?

Happy Wife. Happy Life.

_____

I can show my faith in God by submitting to my spouse.

_____

Wife submit to your husband.

_____

Marriage is 50/50.

_____

Marriage is choosing to say "yes" to my vows every day.

I can choose my mother over my wife.

I can choose my children over my spouse.

I am trapped.

I can love my wife because God told me to.

My spouse's behavior does not dictate my obedience to God.

That woman You gave me.

How I feel does not stop me from loving my wife.

If I'm in a bad mood, I can say anything to my family.

My husband is broke. I can leave him.

Adding my faith to my spouse's produces much fruit.

How can we walk together, except we agree?

Marriage is hard.

Division in our house causes destruction.

Relationships are hard.

Communication is hard.

If I don't do it, it won't get done.

If I don't do it, it won't be done right.

My spouse is now terminally ill. I can leave the marriage.

We have a disabled child. I did not sign up for this, so I can leave the marriage.

Division in our house is disobedience.

My spouse is now disabled. I can leave the marriage.

God's grace is sufficient for me.

In my weakness, God's strength is made perfect.

As a husband, I am required to lead my family.

I am required to take care of my home.

God's grace is sufficient for this marriage.

I am allowed to be honest about my thoughts about a thing.

I can ask for help.

I can have sex with anyone I like during my marriage.

My spouse's body changed. I'm going to leave.

My attitude does not dictate my actions.

I can throw a verbal gut punch.

Marriage is honorable.

It's better to ask for forgiveness rather than ask for permission.

What we both agree to is allowed.

I can cry to get my way.

I can live my truth.

The marriage bed is undefiled.

A little sarcasm is acceptable.

I am allowed to say no regarding sex.

I can speak my truth

We can dishonor God even in our marriage bed.

A white lie is good if I'm sparing my spouse's feelings.

I can do whatever I like to my spouse's body.

My body is not my own, but my spouse's.

My spouse is broke. I'm outta here.

A little lie is ok.

My spouse is a gift.

What's yours is mine and what's mine is mine.

Appendix 3

Ecclesiastes 4:9-12

Read Ecclesiastes 4:9-12. The purpose of this exercise is to create a physical representation of your relationship and strengthen the concept you have of marriage. We want you to go away from this with a lasting memento of how special your marriage is in the kingdom of God. We hope your view of marriage aligns more with the way God sees it.

Step 1: Choose Your Color

Husband, choose a color: red, yellow, or blue.
Your color selection should be different from your wife's.
Your selection will remain the same throughout this activity.

What color did you select? _____

Wife, choose a color: red, yellow, or blue)
Your color selection should be different from your husband's.
Your selection will be yours throughout this activity.

What color did you select? _____

Step 2: Gather Your Supplies

- Supplies:
- Scissors
- Ruler or tape measure
- 1 package pipe cleaners, any color
- 1 skein white yarn
- 1 skein yarn in the husband's color
- 1 skein yarn in the wife's color
- 2 skeins yarn in the color resulting from the husband and wife's colors being mixed

If the husband selected blue and the wife selected red, buy 2 skeins of purple yarn because red and blue together create purple.
.

Step 3: Cut Your Individual Yarn

Using the suggested information below in "Chart A: Individual His/Hers," consider the roles you play and the time spend living your life. Are you a sorority sister? Are you a basketball coach? These are examples of the roles you might play. Did you go to a family reunion, last summer? Do you plan to attend a local concert this month? These are examples of the time you spend living your life. Take the time to decide on each. Some examples are provided. There is space for you to add your own.

a. Partners should cut one 36" string to represent each <u>role</u> they play in life. For example: if the wife is a daughter, sister, friend, and employee, she will cut four 36" strings of yarn in the color she selected. The husband will do the same for his roles.

b. Partners should cut one 36" string to represent each way they spend their time. For example: If the husband goes to the gym (Physical activity), cuts the grass, washes the car (household duties), and goes to work (employment), he will cut four 36" strings of yarn in the color she selected. The wife will do the same for her roles.

c. Make a pile of yarn for each partner.

d. Hold up the yarn pieces at the center. Using a pipe cleaner, tie all of them together. There should be 2 separate pipe cleaners. One for Him and one for Her.

Step 4: Cut Your Foundation Yarn

Read Matthew 7:24-27. The white yarn represents the foundation of your marriage. It is the bedrock upon which you are building (have built) this relationship. Every marriage is built on the assurance that the unshakeable foundation will provide longevity.

Despite the severity of the winds and waves that come, a sure foundation is what will carry you through.

a. Cut 15 pieces of white yarn 6 feet long.

b. Hold up all the pieces of white yarn at the center. Using a pipe cleaner, tie them together.

Step 5: Cut Your One Cord Yarn

Using the suggested information below in "Chart B: We Are One Cord," discuss the roles and time spent that you and your spouse are currently living as a married couple. In other words, my family dynamic includes biological parents, step-parents, as well as grandparents for each. We are a big group! This makes my "Extended family quality time" double the average "How I spend my time." Discuss your dynamic with your spouse as you decide how many One Cord strings you genuinely need. Take extra time with this. The idea is that you both objectively approach your union which unites each of your family dynamics. Each role matters. Each time demand matters. As you progress, you may discover additional roles or time demands. Write them down on the chart. If you need more space, use the margins to capture, completely, your thought process before cutting.

a. Pick up the blended color. The blended color is your "One Cord" color. Remember this color is the combination of your individually selected colors from earlier.

b. Cut the One Cord yarn. Each One Cord string should be 6 feet (72"). Per the Chart B: "Role" and "Time" selections you made, cut that number of 6-foot (72") One Cord strings. (Example: if together, 25 different "Role" and "Time" selections were made, cut 25 6-foot (72") One Cord strings.

c. Hold up the One Cord yarn at the center. Using a pipe cleaner, tie all the One Cord strings together.

Step 6: The Beginning of Your One Cord

At this point, you should have 4 pipe cleaners tying different parts of your One Cord

a. Spouse #1: Hold up all the One Cord parts together in one hand. What do you see at this point? Is it a lot of yarn? Is it kind of small? If you think you've left out something, go back and discuss your roles and time spent more thoroughly.

Reflect together on what you see. Do the strings accurately reflect who you are and how you spend your time as individuals? If not, make adjustments.

Chart A: Individual His/Hers

Role You Play	Time Spent
Mother/Father	Work/Income
Brother/Sister	Physical Activity
Son/Daughter	Parenting
Auntie/Uncle	Writing
Pastor	Music
5-Fold	Education
	Studying the word
	Prayer
	Worship
	Cooking
	Cleaning
	Personal care
	Watching TV

Chart B: We Are One Cord Foundation

God	Jesus
Holy Spirit	Trust
Friendship	Love
Respect	Financial Fidelity
Emotional Fidelity	Physical Fidelity
Financial Discipline	Accepting Accountability
Communication	Honesty
Submission	

Chart B: We Are One Cord

Role You Play	Time Spent
Husband/Wife	Prayer
Mother/Father	Worship
Coach	Studying the Word
Teacher	Quality time together
Pastor	Time with each child
Disciplinarian	Extended Family Time
Taxi Driver	Landscaping
Advocate	Time with kids
Chef	Dinner at grandma's
Housekeeper	Family reunion
Accountant	Parenting
Money Manager	Intimacy
Buyer	Spiritual Intimacy
Referee	Work/Income
Judge	
Planner	
Travel Agent	

Chart B: We Are One Cord

Role You Play	Time Spent
Landscaper	
Mechanic	

Step 7: Braid Your One Cord

This step will take both of you as we expect your One Cord is probably massive. One spouse will hold up the yarn, while the other spouse will braid. Choose your roles wisely.

a. With Spouse #1 holding up the One Cord by the pipe cleaners, Spouse #2 will carefully braid all the strings including all the colors and all the foundation. Take your time. If you find a string hanging free, go back and braid it in. No strings should be left hanging loose.

Step 8: Seal your One Cord

a. Spouse # 1 might be a bit tired of holding up the One Cord. Additionally, Spouse #2 might be tired of braiding. Don't quit! You're doing great work!

a.Spouse #2 take a pipe cleaner (or as many as you need tied together) and seal your One Cord. Again, no strings should be left hanging loose. If you find yourself unable to seal, add more pipe cleaners until you are successful.

Step 9: Record your One Cord

a.Take a picture of your One Cord. This is what your relationship looks like at its best. Tiring and difficult, this massive braid shows you how much you two do together and individually. There is no damage. There are no flaws. Your meticulous, unified work is what God sees for your marriage. This braid cannot be easily broken. Did you realize how much work goes into what you have? Did you count the costs of these demands? Was there a particular Role or Time Spent you decided to add later? Did you discover Roles or Time Spent that you should eliminate? What have you learned about your relationship thus far?

Record your thoughts here.

Step 10: Test Your One Cord

The beautiful period in your relationship represented by your newly created amalgamation of color is your "honeymoon phase". All is right with the world. You love the idea of waking next to your new spouse. You find random love note stickies on your bathroom mirror. You get up a little bit earlier, put on make-up, and curl your hair. The idea of cooking an elaborate breakfast complete with tiny fruit tarts, and eggs benedict, makes you giddy. You remember that time. Don't you? If you're currently in your honeymoon phase, enjoy! It is a time to be cherished and, if possible, prolonged into perpetuity. Hold tightly to those flowery, sugary sweet thoughts because we are transitioning to rough waters.

We are going to make some demands of your One Cord. Let's see if she can stay afloat. Pick up the scissors.

Place your One Cord on a flat surface. Because we care about your mindset during this exercise, we will offer two hypothetical situations that will damage the solidity of your relationship. Remember: you are NOT opponents. One additional note: These scenarios are based on all participants being believers.

Situation 1: After dating for 12 months, and early in your new marriage, Wife discovered that Husband's income was, and remains substantially less than he'd previously admitted. In other words, He lied.

a. Take your time discussing the damage. You will find suggestions listed below. But perhaps, you agree upon additional damage. Write them in the area provided. Carefully cut the cords that are trust, financial fidelity, income, provider, honesty, and any additional cords you decide are also damaged.

The chart will tell you if these are His, Hers, Foundation, or One Cord. Cut the appropriate string one at a time. We do this carefully so that no collateral damage occurs

Suggested damage:
Trust (Foundation)
Financial Fidelity (Foundation)
Work/Income (His, One Cord)
Provider (One Cord)
Honesty (Foundation)

Mutually agreed upon damage: (List all that you decide upon.)

Situation 2: Wife's mom is coming into town for a visit. She wants to stay at your home. Husband disagrees. He wants her to stay in a hotel because he wants more quality time with Wife. Husband is willing to pay for half of Mother-in-Law's hotel stay as a gesture of good faith. Mother-in-law accuses son-in-law of isolating her daughter.

a. Take your time discussing the damage. You will find suggestions listed below. But perhaps, you agree upon additional damage. Write them in the area provided. Carefully cut the cords that are referee, communication, quality time, extended family quality time, and any additional cords you decide are also damaged. The chart will tell you if these are His, Hers, Foundation, or One Cord. Cut the appropriate string one at a time. We do this carefully so that no collateral damage occurs.

Suggested damage:
Referee
Communication
Quality Time
Extended Family Quality Time

Mutually agreed upon damage: (List all that you decide upon.)

_____
_____
_____
_____
_____
_____

Step 11: Record Your One Cord

a. Take a picture of your One Cord. This is what your relationship looks like at its worst.

Step 12: Expect Repairs – A Practical Approach

If you drop a television and the screen gets cracked, do you try to glue the cracks together? How well will that picture be for you? Chances are, you won't be able to see anything with all that glue in place. What are you going to do with it? I would throw it away in the nearest dumpster and go get a new one. But that is NOT what we are going to do with your One Cord. Jesus expects repairs when He tells us in both Matthew 19:6 and Mark 10:8-9 that no one can separate that which God has joined together. Do not discard what God has joined. This step is where we do the work that is repairing damage taken by the previous hypothetical situations. Repairing is a two-step process. First, forgive and seek forgiveness. Then, let go. Let's look at each situation once more.

Situation 1: After dating for 12 months, and early in your new marriage, Wife discovered that Husband's income was, and remains substantially less than he'd previously admitted. In other words, He lied. In a fit of frustration, Wife yelled at Husband for an hour.

Forgive.

Forgive. Even if Husband
1. has not accepted responsibility for the lie.
2. has not accepted accountability for the lie.
3. has not apologized for the lie.
4. has not offered a plan to satisfy the budgetary shortages.

Forgive him.

Forgive. Even if Wife
1. fails to show remorse.
2. fails to apologize for her uncontrolled anger.
fails to acknowledge her responsibility in the lie

Forgive her.

Whenever you stand praying, if you have anything against anyone, forgive him [drop the issue, let it go], so that your Father who is in heaven will also forgive you your transgressions and wrongdoings [against Him and others]. [But if you do not forgive, neither will your Father in heaven forgive your transgressions."] Mark 11:25-26 AMP

Seek forgiveness.

Husband: Seek Wife's forgiveness.

Wife: Seek Husband's forgiveness.

Seek forgiveness.

"If a brother sins against you, go to him privately and confront him with his fault. If he listens and confesses it, you have won back a brother. Matthew 18:15 AMP

Pay attention and always be on guard [looking out for one another]! If your brother sins and disregards God's precepts, solemnly warn him; and if he repents and changes, forgive him. Even if he sins against you seven times a day, and returns to you seven times and says, 'I repent,' you must forgive him [that is, give up resentment and consider the offense recalled and annulled]." Luke 17:3-4 AMP

Let go. "Life is an accumulation of learning. A baby does not forget how to crawl when they learn to walk. They simply learn a better way to get from point A to point B." D. Gipson.

What does letting go look like for your marriage? Together, with fasting and praying, ask God for a better strategy or approach. Ask God for wisdom, on how to renew the mind of your marriage Ask God for the knowledge on what about the mind of your marriage needs renewal. Ask God, also, for the understanding of when renewal begins and how long that renewal will take.

Let go.

Let go. Husband must let go of
1. shame
2. Wife's emotional outburst

Husband must repent of
1. lying

Let go. Wife must let go of
1. anger
2. resentment

Wife must repent of
1. not remaining steadfast during difficult times
2. being easily angered
3. being rude
4. failing to honor Husband as lord of the house

Or rude. It does not demand its own way. It is not irritable, and it keeps no record of being wronged. 1 Corinthians 13:5 NLT

Situation 2: Wife's mom is coming into town for a visit. She wants to stay at your home. Husband disagrees. He wants her to stay in a hotel because he wants more quality time with Wife. Husband is willing to pay for half of Mother-in-Law's hotel stay as a gesture of good faith. Mother-in-law accuses son-in-law of isolating her daughter.

Forgive.

Forgive. Even if Wife
1. is still indifferent
2. has made no decision

Forgive her.

Forgive. Even if Husband
1. is still lacking compassion
2. is still insensitive
3. is still lacking understanding

Forgive him.

Forgive. Even if Mother-in-law
1. is still being pushy
2. is still lacking compassion
3. is making accusations about your marriage
4. is still lacking understanding

Forgive Mother-in-law.

Reread Mark 11:25-26 AMP.

Seek Forgiveness.

Husband: Seek Wife's & Mother-in-law's forgiveness.

Wife: Seek Husband's & Mother's forgiveness.

Mother-in-law: Seek daughter's & son-in-law's forgiveness.

Seek forgiveness. (Matthew 18:15 AMP, Luke 17:3-4 AMP)

Let go. "Dying to self, you will always look like Christ." W. Tillis. What does letting go look like for your marriage and your relationship with your external family? Together, with fasting and praying, ask God for a better strategy or approach. Ask God for wisdom, on how to better prepare for future interactions with your extended family. Ask God for the knowledge on what other strategies can be put into practice. Ask God, also, for the understanding of when to embrace and when to refrain from embracing.

Let go.

Let go. Wife must let go of
1. being put in the middle as a referee
2. Mother's persistence
3. Husband's persistence

Wife must repent of
1. Not honoring Husband as lord of the house

Let go. Husband must let go of
1. wife's indifference
2. Mother-in-law's persistence

Husband must repent of
1. Lack of understanding
2. Lack of compassion
3. For being self-seeking

Let go. Mother-in-law must let go of
1. Her daughter
2. Her own way

Mother-in-law must repent of
1. Not looking for the best in son-in-law
2. Insisting on her own way
3. For being self-seeking
4. Accusing son-in-law

Let go. (1 Corinthians 13)

Step 13: Repairing Your One Cord

Your bruised, battered, and damaged One Cord remains on the table. The injuries sustained represent the impact of the storms you and your spouse have, and will, endure. The beauty once held is dulled. You may be discouraged. In this step, we offer this, your marriage, to Jehovah Rapha who can heal any disease; resolve any conflict; and reanimate any dead thing. Allow His powerful hand to remold and reshape your fractured marriage. All it takes is faith. If you believe it possible, He will exceed your wildest imaginations.

The top of your One Cord is where you held the yarn while it was being braided. As you make repairs, the side of the damaged cord closest to the top is the side where the repairs always begin. You must forgive and seek forgiveness, first. And immediately after, you must let go.

One of you will hold the top and bottom sides of the damage in either hand. Make sure you are holding the same cord. While the other of you will tie pipe cleaners on both sides. Remember to always begin with the top side of the damage. Pipe cleaner color does not matter. The repair does.

Step 14: Record Your One Cord

a. Take a picture of your One Cord. This is what your relationship looks like after you give it to God. It is not as it was initially. But it is now stronger than ever.

One Cord

Check-in and Celebrate!

How have we grown in the past year?

Before "The Winning Series: Marriage", describe the flight path of your relationship. Was it on autopilot? Was it in a nosedive? Was it in extreme turbulence? Were you just boarding? As you consider these ideas, Reflect on the following.

One month after completing "Winning," detail ways your relationship has grown. _____
_____
_____
_____
_____
_____
_____
_____

Six months after completing "Winning," detail ways your relationship has grown. _____
_____
_____
_____
_____
_____
_____

Congratulations! You have completed "The Winning Series: Marriage!"
It's time to celebrate!

www.ingramcontent.com/pod-product-compliance
Lightning Source LLC
Chambersburg PA
CBHW072117050526
44107CB00098BA/320